P9-CLO-023

LEGO NINJAGO
Masters of Spinjitzu

OFFICIAL GUIDE

BY GREG FARSHTEY

SCHOLASTIC INC.
NEW YORK   TORONTO   LONDON   AUCKLAND
SYDNEY   MEXICO CITY   NEW DELHI   HONG KONG

No part of this publication may be reproduced in whole or in part, or stored in a retrieval system, or transmitted in any form or by any means, electronic, mechanical, photocopying, recording, or otherwise, without written permission of the publisher. For information regarding permission, write to Scholastic Inc., Attention: Permissions Department, 557 Broadway, New York, NY 10012.

ISBN 978-0-545-38285-4

LEGO, the LEGO logo, the Brick and the Knob configurations and the Minifigure are trademark of the LEGO Group. ©2011 The LEGO Group. Produced by Scholastic Inc. under license from the LEGO Group.
Published by Scholastic Inc. SCHOLASTIC and associated logos are trademarks and/or registered trademarks of Scholastic Inc.

12 11 10 9 8 7 6 5 4 3 2 1   11 12 13 14 15 16/0

Printed in China
This edition first printing, September 2011

CONTENTS

My name is **Sensei Wu**. This world, **Ninjago**, was once a paradise. Now it is under siege by the forces of darkness . . . and there are few brave enough to fight for right. If you are one of those who would defend **Ninjago**, then I welcome you.

I have written this book to help you understand this world, its **heroes**, and the **villains** who would conquer it. Within these pages, you will learn secrets I have shared with very, very few over the centuries. These secrets are powerful and dangerous in the wrong hands, so you must be both wise and courageous to possess them.

Now it is time for you to begin your **journey**. Inside this volume, you will meet my brave ninja, and the terrible skeleton warriors they must fight. You will learn of the power of **Spinjitzu** and the Golden Weapons that threaten the very existence of **Ninjago**. To begin, it is best that I tell you some of the history of this world. . . .

The Legend of Ninjago

In ancient times, the first **Master of Spinjitzu** created the world of Ninjago. He was a being of infinite wisdom and power, just and fair, a father to this planet just as he was a father to two sons. My brother, Garmadon, and I both grew up in his shadow, hoping to someday be all that he was.

There are some who can dream of being great men in the future, and that dream can sustain their spirit. There are others who become convinced they can never achieve their goal. In their hearts, the desire to be someone others will admire gets twisted into no more than a bitter lust for power. My brother looked at our father and saw all the things he felt he could never be. In time, he came to hate me, my father, and Ninjago itself.

Our father left us a legacy. He had created the Four Weapons of Spinjitzu—the Scythe of Quakes, the Shurikens of Ice, the Nunchuks of Lightning, and the Dragon Sword of Fire. When he died, he left the Weapons

LEGO NINJAGO
Masters of Spinjitzu

under the protection of me and Garmadon. The two of us vowed to give our lives to keep the Weapons safe.

Garmadon broke that vow. He wanted the Weapons for himself. When I caught him trying to steal them, we fought. I was victorious, and Garmadon was banished to the Underworld.

Following the battle, I hid the four Weapons in the far corners of Ninjago. I then had an old and trusted friend create a map to their locations and hide it well. I believed the Weapons to be as safe as they could be.

I was wrong. My brother allied with the king of the Underworld, Samukai, and launched a plan to seize the Weapons.

Samukai's skeleton warriors invaded Ninjago, stole the map, and began a search for the powerful artifacts. Knowing that I could not stop this myself, I recruited four young men to become ninja. With their help, I hope to be able to defeat my brother for a second—and final—time.

I have trained them and taught them as best I could in a short time. I have made it possible for them to discover the power of Spinjitzu within themselves. Now I can only hope I have given them enough, and that they are strong enough to overcome the challenges they will face.

Their lives and the life of this planet depend upon it.

CHARACTERS

The world of **Ninjago** is divided.

On one side are **Garmadon** and his evil **Underworld** forces.

On the other, those of us willing to fight him with the power of **Spinjitzu**.

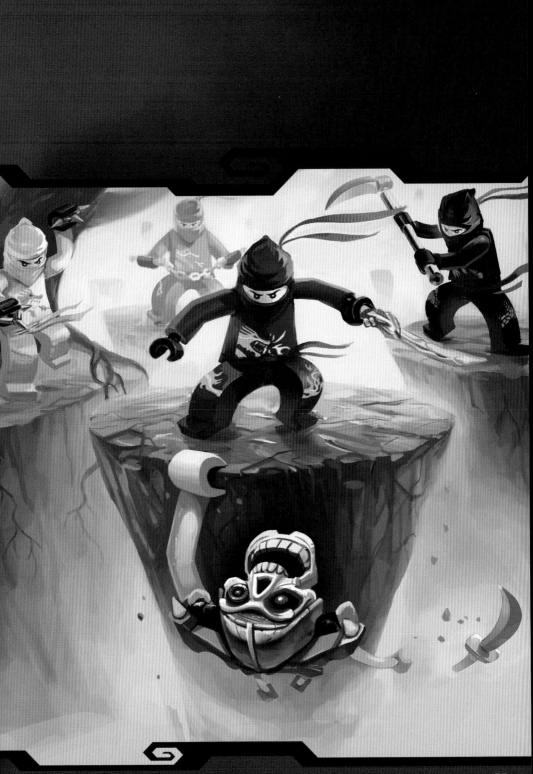

Kai

Brave, reckless, daring, stubborn, inspiring, infuriating—all of these describe Kai, the Ninja of Fire. Of all my ninja, he was the most difficult to train . . . not because he lacked the skill, but because he lacked patience and was reluctant to listen to anyone else. Still, I saw potential in him. He has speed and grace, both of which helped him to master Spinjitzu.

I see much of his father in Kai. He is devoted to his sister, Nya, as his father was devoted to both son and daughter. Given time, I think Kai will carve out a legend for himself as the greatest warrior for right Ninjago has ever known.

ELEMENT:	Fire
WEAPON:	Dragon Sword of Fire
FAVORITE NINJA MOVE:	Falcon Flame Strike
FAVORITE FOOD:	Hamburgers
HOBBIES:	Music, breakdancing, blacksmithing
QUOTE:	"You guys looked like you could use some fun."

NINJA NOTES:

- Kai was the last of the four ninja recruited by Sensei Wu.

- His father was Sensei Wu's oldest and most trusted friend.

- Kai and his sister, Nya, run a blacksmith shop in their village called 4 Weapons.

Cole

There is no physical challenge Cole cannot overcome. Whether it's climbing the highest mountain, swimming across the sea, or hiking through dense jungle, Cole has done it. But what he has always wanted most is the chance to use his strength and skill for a good cause. I offered him that chance.

Now he is the leader of my ninja team. Keeping the others united and focused on the mission is a difficult task. Fortunately, Cole is smart, steady, and calm. He knows when to give orders and when to let his partners follow their instincts. Under his guidance, the team has defeated frightening foes and done

ELEMENT:	Earth
WEAPON:	Scythe of Quakes
FAVORITE NINJA MOVE:	Power Earth Slam
FAVORITE COLOR:	Black
HOBBIES:	Rock climbing
QUOTE:	"We're a team. It's time to start acting like it."

things no one would have thought possible. From people like Cole, I expect nothing less.

NINJA NOTES:

▲ Sensei Wu first met Cole when the young man was climbing the highest mountain on Ninjago, one no one had ever scaled before. Cole was surprised to find Sensei Wu waiting for him at the top.

▲ In the past, Cole was always trying to do dangerous tasks on his own. Now he has learned the importance of working in a team, and is trying to teach this to the others.

▲ Cole believes in doing as much planning as possible and often doesn't sleep the night before a battle.

Zane

My Ninja of Ice is perhaps the most mysterious member of our team. Zane has no memory of his past and is plagued by secrets he fears he will never learn. He is brilliant but seems distant from the other ninja, finding it very difficult to join in their laughing and joking.

I first met him when he was meditating at the bottom of a half-frozen lake. He agreed to join the team in hopes that adventuring would lead him to discovering more about his early life. His skill and courage have earned him the respect of his teammates, even if Jay and the others do not always understand him.

ELEMENT:	Ice
WEAPON:	Shurikens of Ice
FAVORITE NINJA MOVE:	Ice Dragon Side Kick
FAVORITE SEASON:	Winter
HOBBIES:	Meditation, snowboarding
QUOTE:	"I do not understand. Was that meant to be humor?"

NINJA NOTES:

✳ Zane has an incredible resistance to cold.

✳ Zane woke up on the outskirts of a village years ago, with no idea of where he came from or how he got there.

✳ Zane tamed the Ice Dragon by making a logical argument to it regarding why an alliance would benefit them both.

Jay

Jay is the Ninja of Lightning and has the same high energy as a bolt of electricity. He moves, thinks, and talks quickly, and always has a joke to break the tension in battle. Of all four ninja, he is the most creative and resourceful.

A skilled inventor, not everything Jay creates always works the way he intends it to. Still, his creations have saved the team more than once. Most recently, by quickly assembling hang gliders out of scraps of material, he enabled the group to escape from a floating city.

ELEMENT:	Lightning
WEAPON:	Nunchuks of Lightning
FAVORITE NINJA MOVE:	Double Forked Lightning Thrust
FAVORITE COLOR:	Blue
HOBBIES:	Inventing, cooking, telling jokes
QUOTE:	"Why was the dragon so tired out? Too many late knights."

NINJA NOTES:

⚡ I first met Jay when he was unsuccessfully testing a pair of homemade wings.

⚡ Jay has a crush on Kai's sister, Nya.

⚡ Jay once created an amplifier for the Lightning Dragon to allow it to roar more loudly.

Sensei Wu

For many, many years, I have been adventuring across the world of **Ninjago**. Using my knowledge of **Spinjitzu**, I have defended the innocent from threats from this world and beyond. All the while, I have feared the day my evil brother, Garmadon, would return to threaten all existence once more.

I have fought many battles and won many victories, but my life has been a lonely one. Now I have my team of ninja, four young men of great courage and heart, dedicated to fighting for justice. **Together, we will strive to bring peace to Ninjago.**

ELEMENTS:	All
WEAPON:	Staff
FAVORITE DRINK:	Tea
HOBBIES:	Adventuring, ninja training
QUOTE:	"There are some powers no man can hope to control . . . or should ever dare try to use."

NINJA NOTES:

- Son of the first Spinjitzu Master.
- First hid the Four Weapons of Spinjitzu ages ago and placed dragons to guard them.
- Master of the Power of Creation.

Nya

Nya is the sister of Kai. When Samukai's skeleton warriors attacked their village, Nya was kidnapped. My brother, Garmadon, no doubt has plans for her . . . perhaps he hopes to use her in some way against Kai. Fear for a loved one's safety can be a powerful weapon.

But Garmadon may well have bitten off more than he can chew. Though she has no ninja training, everything I have heard is that Nya is quite able to take care of herself. Garmadon may have thought he was abducting a frail flower, only to find he has a raging tigress in his midst.

WEAPON:	Daggers
FAVORITE FOOD:	Pizza with pepperoni and bananas
HOBBIES:	Blacksmithing, gymnastics
QUOTE:	"I can take care of myself. I don't need protecting."

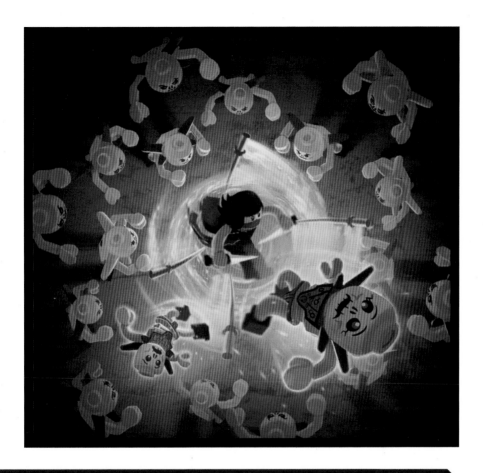

NINJA NOTES:

- ❌ Nya is more practical than Kai and often has to keep his feet on the ground and his temper in check.
- ❌ Does not know Spinjitzu or any formal martial arts, but has a fighting style that is uniquely her own.
- ❌ Nya is actually a better blacksmith than Kai, but prefers not to point that out to him.

Garmadon

Garmadon could have been an adventurer like me, a fighter for right, perhaps even a greater hero than I could ever hope to be. But he let greed and his lust for power set him against me. When our battle was done, he had been exiled from this plane of existence. But in all the many years since, he must have been plotting his revenge.

Cunning, crafty, and powerful, Garmadon always has schemes within schemes. Even his ally, Samukai, is never certain what he may be planning. One can only be sure that whatever his plot, it promises fear and destruction for all who live.

ELEMENT:	All
WEAPON:	Varies
FAVORITE COLOR:	Black
HOBBIES:	Planning escape and revenge against Sensei Wu; lying and deceiving
QUOTE:	"Everything is going according to plan . . . but, ah, which plan? That is what you cannot know."

NINJA NOTES:

- At one time, Garmadon adventured by my side, battling evil.
- Garmadon's ambition is to remake Ninjago in his own image.
- Although I have recruited my ninja to help me, I consider defeating Garmadon to ultimately be my responsibility.

Samukai

After Garmadon, **Samukai is easily the most vile and dangerous enemy of the ninja**. Where most skeletons are simply jealous of the living, Samukai actually hates anyone who is alive. Ruler of the Underworld and the skeleton legion, he struck an alliance with Garmadon to invade and crush the world of Ninjago.

Unlike his servants, Samukai is not at all slow or dull-witted. He's a brilliant leader who keeps his army in line through fear. His four arms make him a devastating hand-to-hand-to-hand-to-hand combatant. He has no mercy, no compassion, no hint of any human feeling. Samukai is ruthless and relentless and a challenge even for me, the powerful Sensei Wu.

WEAPON:	Varies, uses up to four at one time
BEST FIGHTING MOVE:	Four-handed fracture
FAVORITE PET:	A venomous fire slug
HOBBIES:	Conquest
QUOTE:	"You are powerful, Garmadon. But never forget who rules this place with four iron fists."

NINJA NOTES:

- ⊛ Samukai is the only skeleton able to fight with four weapons at once.
- ⊛ Just as power-hungry as Garmadon, it's impossible to predict how long their alliance will last.
- ⊛ Prior to Garmadon's betrayal, we fought and defeated Samukai together.

Kruncha

Kruncha is a strong skeleton warrior. He can plow through a brick wall or smash a boulder using just his fist. In a fight, his strategy is to just keep pounding until his opponent is worn out.

His weakness is that he lacks intelligence. In fact, some of the boulders he hits are smarter than he is. Kruncha has been known to mistake rocks for food and bite into them. He slowed the skeletons' search for the Scythe of Quakes because he was reading the map upside down. Still, his sheer strength makes him very dangerous.

WEAPON:	Varies
BEST FIGHTING MOVE:	Bone-bruiser bash
FAVORITE FOOD:	Donuts
BEST FRIEND:	Nuckal (though Nuckal wouldn't agree)
HOBBIES:	Eating, fighting, then eating some more
QUOTE:	"Huh? What?"

NINJA NOTES:

- 💀 Zane once tricked Kruncha into believing he had not seen the ninja when he actually had.
- 💀 Usually gets assignments that require strength, but not brains.
- 💀 Once destroyed an ancient ninja fortress by eating it for lunch.

Chopov is the chief mechanic of Samukai's skeleton legion. It's his job to keep the Turbo Shredder and other vehicles in perfect working order. To Chopov, that means, "If something isn't working, smash it with your machete until it does."

In battle, Chopov likes to cheat. He will pretend to be defeated and strike when his opponent's back is turned, throw dirt in his enemy's eyes, or shout "Look behind you!" in the middle of a fight. His tactics are foul, but unfortunately they do work for him.

WEAPON:	Machete
BEST FIGHTING MOVE:	Skull smash
FAVORITE SPORT:	Bone rolling
LEAST FAVORITE ACTIVITY:	Following rules
HOBBIES:	Driving, tinkering
QUOTE:	"It's not working. Let me hit it a few times."

NINJA NOTES:

- Chopov secretly hopes Bonezai will get captured and he will be put in charge of designing vehicles.

- His one attempt at creating a vehicle on his own—the Turbo Turtle—did not work out so well.

- Chopov once took the Skull Motorbike apart and wound up with leftover parts when he put it back together. He threw them away and hopes Bonezai never finds out.

Krazi

Krazi is well named, as he is completely mad. He is extremely dangerous in battle, because he is totally unpredictable. One day, he may fight ferociously for hours, and another day he may sneak away at the start of a fight and then come back and strike later.

Even Samukai finds it difficult to keep Krazi under control. He was almost left behind in the Underworld, but he is too formidable a fighter not to have along. All my ninja know to beware if they see him coming. . . .

WEAPON:	Bone club
BEST FIGHTING MOVE:	Knee-bone spring strike
FAVORITE SPORT:	Mountain smashing
HOBBIES:	Screaming, running, biting trees
QUOTE:	"Ha! You have me right where I want you!"

NINJA NOTES:

- Krazi once got into a fight with his own shadow in the Underworld that lasted for three days.

- He does not believe in taking prisoners.

- Krazi is always volunteering to have Bonezai test his new weapon designs on him, although Samukai has forbidden this.

Nuckal

Nuckal is one of Samukai's field commanders. Slightly smarter than the average skeleton warrior, it's his job to keep Kruncha, Krazi, and the rest in line. This is extremely difficult, as most skeletons go wild once out of the Underworld and can be hard to keep focused on their mission.

Impatient, short-tempered, and nasty, Nuckal enforces discipline with a hard rap on the skull. He knows that if the skeleton legion fails in its job, he is going to get the blame. That could make it a long, long time before he gets to leave the Underworld again.

WEAPON:	Bone axe
BEST FIGHTING MOVE:	Leg-bone lightning lash
FAVORITE FOOD:	Brussels-sprout yogurt
HOBBIES:	Shouting, smacking warriors on the head
QUOTE:	"Put the cow down and get back to work!

NINJA NOTES:

- Nuckal does not trust Garmadon at all and fears this mission may result in the destruction of the skeleton legion.
- He once took on Frakjaw and Krazi at the same time and beat them both.
- Nuckal has a secret respect for Cole, believing that as leaders they both face the same pressures.

Bonezai

Bonezai designs and builds the vehicles used by the skeleton army. Although he might not seem very bright, he is a genius at creating wheeled engines of destruction. He's still relatively new at his job—he's only been doing it 5,000 years now—but he's already made the Skeleton Monster Truck, the Turbo Shredder, and many more. He's hoping to move on to flying vehicles soon.

Surprisingly mild-mannered for a skeleton, Bonezai can be pretty easy to get along with . . . unless, of course, you get a smudge on one of his vehicles or, worse, put a dent in one. Then Bonezai flies into a rage. The last skeleton to put a scratch in the Turbo Shredder wound up being turned into a tool rack.

WEAPON:	Pickaxe
BEST FIGHTING MOVE:	Shinbone shove
FAVORITE PLACE:	His workshop in the Underworld
HOBBIES:	Engineering
QUOTE:	"I don't care what you do, just don't dent it."

NINJA NOTES:

- Bonezai test-drives all his vehicles, usually at high speed.
- He is working hard on coming up with more weapons designed specifically for fighting ninja.
- Bonezai can be easily distracted in a fight by doing damage to one of his vehicles.

Wyplash

One would think that a walking skeleton would be difficult to miss. Yet Wyplash has made himself valuable to Samukai as a spy, somehow able to gather information on Ninjago villages without being caught.

He is a master of stealth. If there is a shadow, no matter how narrow, it seems Wyplash can vanish into it. He moves in complete silence, easier to do when one does not have to breathe. His senses are sharp, allowing him to read documents or hear conversations from far away. When there is no work for him as a spy, he is used as a scout.

WEAPON:	Varies
BEST FIGHTING MOVE:	The Wyplash whip kick
FAVORITE TACTIC:	Attacking from behind
HOBBIES:	Sneaking
QUOTE:	"They never knew I was there."

NINJA NOTES:

- Wyplash was the one who discovered that the map to the Four Weapons of Spinjitzu was hidden in Kai's shop.

- He has already clashed more than once with Cole, who has made a vow to bring Wyplash down.

- Wyplash is so good at staying hidden that most of his fellow skeletons are never sure when he's around.

Frakjaw

The most amazing thing about Frakjaw is that he is still alive, if you can call an animated skeleton "alive." **Frakjaw never shuts up—ever—no matter the situation.** Add that he has the unusual talent to be able to spot Wyplash and one can see where problems might occur. He almost ruined one of Wyplash's missions by striking up a loud conversation.

Samukai, however, is not stupid and rapidly discovered how to use Frakjaw to his advantage: He makes a good guard. In addition, his constant talking attracts attention and can be used to lure ninja into a trap. I have had to teach my team to try and ignore him.

WEAPON:	Mace ball
BEST FIGHTING MOVE:	Perpetual patter punch
FAVORITE SPORT:	Debate
HOBBIES:	Talking . . . talking . . . and talking
QUOTE:	"And then I said to him, what do you mean I talk too much? Why, I've never been accused of such a thing. It's just silly, I mean, how could a being talk too much? The very idea —"

NINJA NOTES:

- Frakjaw once talked for 47 hours straight.
- Bonezai has been known to ask Frakjaw to test vehicles he suspects might explode.
- Being assigned to live near Frakjaw in the Underworld is considered to be a punishment.

DRAGONS

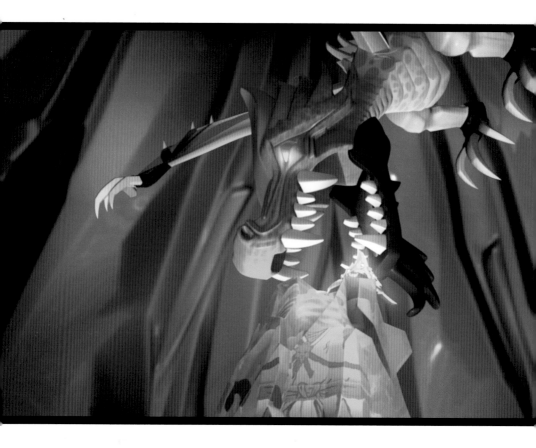

The four most powerful allies of the ninja are the elemental dragons they meet in their adventures. The Ice Dragon, Earth Dragon, Fire Dragon, and Lightning Dragon are powerful flying creatures and the only beings able to move easily between this world and the Underworld.

Dragons are some of the most mysterious residents of Ninjago. It is known that they are not native to the planet, or even the dimension, but no one knows exactly where they do

come from. It's also not known if the dragons are good or evil. It may be that they are neither, but rather are simply willing to work with those few humans they trust.

When I hid the Four Weapons of Spinjitzu, I sought out the four elemental dragons to ask them to protect the artifacts. The dragons agreed, on one condition: I could never ask anything more of them. They would guard the Weapons against anyone who tried to steal them, and that would include me and my allies. For that reason, when the four ninja went to retrieve the Weapons, they found themselves pursued by the dragons.

Although each dragon is very different, they all have some things in common. Each dragon has a breath weapon connected to their element (breathing fire, ice, etc.). They also have scales which act as natural armor, and sharp claws and teeth. All dragons have wings, though how well they fly differs. The most amazing thing about dragons is that they are able to move between worlds, carrying the ninja from Ninjago to the Underworld and back in their first adventure together.

Many mysteries remain about dragons. Are these the only four in existence? Is it possible that other dragons exist, associated with other elements? If so, are these dragons also willing to fight for right, or are they enemies of humanity? Only time will tell.

Ice Dragon

Eldest and wisest of the four dragons, the Ice Dragon is a powerful elemental being.
Although fierce and ferocious, it is capable of understanding and reason. Its first concern is protection of the golden Shuriken of Ice, a job it has done for many thousands of years. Its second is preservation of the dragon species as a whole. Anything that threatens the world of Ninjago is seen by this beast as a threat to its species as well.

The Ice Dragon is capable of breathing sub-zero air which instantly freezes any moisture in the air, making it appear as if the creature breathes ice. Its body contains an extra layer of insulation to protect it from the frigid environment in which it lives as well as its own power. Its scales are metallic and gleam so brightly that they can cause ice blindness in bright sunlight.

Dwelling in the frozen northern provinces, the Ice Dragon's lair could be reached only by sailing across a dangerous sea filled with icebergs. Few mariners could survive the trip . . . fewer still would ever make the attempt. The legends of the Ice Dragon's power are such that only the very brave or the very foolish would dare risk angering the creature.

DRAGON NOTES:

✱ Although more comfortable in a freezing environment, the Ice Dragon can survive in very hot climates for a short time. After a while, intense heat will begin to weaken it.

✱ The Ice Dragon has been ridden by Zane since he persuaded it that Garmadon is a threat to the world.

✱ The Ice Dragon is a meat-eater, usually feasting on snow serpents, wild frost gators, and any other large prey it can find.

Earth Dragon

The Earth Dragon is physically the strongest of the four dragons. Dwelling in the Caves of Despair, it has thick black scales, massive teeth and claws, and a very short temper. Much of its time is spent asleep and it does not react well to being awakened. It has spent many thousands of years guarding the Scythe of Quakes, and in all that time, no one has tried to steal the Weapon. As a result, the dragon has grown restless and eager for a fight.

Along with its great strength, the Earth Dragon is able to breathe earth and rock, creating its own airborne avalanches. Like all dragons, it can fly, though it is not the most skilled at it due to so many years living underground. The Earth Dragon is attuned to the rhythms of the planet and can sense the coming of earthquakes, disruptions in the environment, or the approach of other living things from miles away.

This creature is an omnivore, capable of eating anything, including rock. Its system is such that it only needs one meal every few thousand years, although that must be a pretty big one. It's said that major quakes have been caused by the Earth Dragon eating away at the faults underground. Whenever the ground shakes, the old and the wise of Ninjago will say, "The Earth Dragon hungers today."

DRAGON NOTES:

▲ The Earth Dragon allies with Cole against Garmadon.

▲ The beast does not fear heat or cold, but does have an intense dislike of water.

▲ The Earth Dragon is revered by farmers, who believe it is responsible for good harvests and rich soil.

Fire Dragon

The most dangerous and potentially destructive of all the dragons, the Fire Dragon dwells in a river of lava within the Temple of Fire. There it guards the Dragon Sword of Fire from any who might try to use its power. Like fire itself, the dragon can be difficult to control—in ancient times, it was known for its rampages.

Everything ever written about the Fire Dragon says the same thing: It cannot be tamed. At best, it can be negotiated with, if you can convince it your cause is just or you have something it wants. Even then, it will not accept orders. It will be an ally but never a servant. Anyone who tries to act like the dragon's master will—if they are lucky—only be dumped off its back from a great height.

The Fire Dragon breathes molten lava. Its scales are crimson and can easily be mistaken for stone.
This creature is immune to heat and flame, but it is vulnerable to extreme cold, and its fights with the Ice Dragon in the past have been legendary.

DRAGON NOTES:

- 🔥 The Fire Dragon was the first to ally with the ninja, after Kai explained the danger posed by Garmadon.

- 🔥 Of the four dragons, the Fire Dragon is the most familiar with the Underworld and can find its way through that region's ever-changing landscape.

- 🔥 The other dragons have, in the past, looked to the Fire Dragon as something of a leader.

Lightning Dragon

Fastest of the four dragons, the Lightning Dragon is also extremely short-tempered, its moods changing as quickly as a flash of the lightning it's named for. It can be a loyal ally or a treacherous foe, all within a few minutes. Its long-time role as guardian of the Nunchuks of Lightning has not made it any friendlier.

The Lightning Dragon lived inside a mysterious floating city, beneath the chamber that housed the Nunchuks. If anyone tried to take the Weapon, it would rise up and use its lightning breath to sizzle them into submission. If need be, it would take flight, moving far faster than anyone would expect something of its great size could do.

The Lightning Dragon has no problem with heat or cold, but like the Fire Dragon and the Earth Dragon, it hates water. It knows it is not the strongest dragon, but its skill and speed make up for that. This beast can strike three times in battle in the time it takes another dragon to strike once.

DRAGON NOTES:

⚡ The Lightning Dragon allows Jay to ride it into battle.

⚡ This creature was the last one to agree to ally with the ninja. Jay had to make it a gift—an amplifier that made its roar louder—before the Lightning Dragon agreed.

⚡ I once said that, like true lightning, the dragon is beautiful, but one must be cautious not to approach too close.

SKELETON VEHICLES

Samukai's skeleton legions ride modern vehicles into their fights against the ninja. Forged in the **Underworld**, these trucks, cycles, and battle cars are designed to overpower enemies and carry the **skeletons** to victory!

Skull Truck

This rolling colossus is crewed by Wyplash and Garmadon but can carry multiple skeleton warriors. Its high suspension and huge wheels allow it to cross the roughest terrain, from the ice fields of the northern provinces to the rocky ground of the Underworld.

The monster truck often leads the way in battle, its super-loud engine and skull grill frightening enemies. The bone spikes on its tires can shred the wheels of any opposing vehicle. Its skull-fist shooter can be used to grab and capture an opponent at long range or wreck buildings. The truck then rolls easily over the rubble.

The skeleton monster truck was designed by Bonezai. It is one of Wyplash's favorite vehicles to modify, which causes a lot of fights with Bonezai, who doesn't like his work messed with. Bonezai once threatened to turn Wyplash's skull into a hood ornament if he didn't stop tinkering with the engine.

WEAPONS:	Skull-fist shooter, bone spikes, bone cages
CREW:	2
MAXIMUM SPEED:	200 mph
ARMOR:	Bone laced with iron
SPECIAL EQUIPMENT:	All-terrain tires, high suspension

Turbo Shredder

The most fearsome vehicle in the skeleton fleet, **the Turbo Shredder is designed for one mission only: pursuit and destruction**. It's fitted with a fanged skull that chomps down as the vehicle moves. Anyone unlucky enough to be caught by the Turbo Shredder is in very serious trouble.

Like the Skeleton Monster Truck, the Turbo Shredder is designed to travel across all terrain. Its large back wheels and tough treads handle rock and ice without a problem. More than once, we have built barriers we thought would stop the Turbo Shredder, only to have it crash right through them.

Bonezai considers the Turbo Shredder his best work so far. On the ground, it is almost unbeatable, which is why my ninja have started trying to attack it from the air while atop their dragons. It's too soon to tell if even the power of the elemental dragons will be able to stop this incredible battle machine.

WEAPONS:	Forward chomper
CREW:	1
MAXIMUM SPEED:	225 mph
ARMOR:	Dragon bone interlaced with Underworld steel
SPECIAL EQUIPMENT:	Treads

Skull Motorbike

One wouldn't think a lone skeleton on a motorcycle would be enough to threaten a trained ninja. Jay didn't think so, either, until he was almost flattened by the Skull Motorbike. Now we all know better and have learned to be wary of the sound of the cycle's elemental engine.

Long and sleek, the motorbike is equipped with a fiendish weapon. As it approaches a target, a device in the front of the cycle is triggered and a slammer arm flies free. It moves so quickly that it doesn't impede the bike's progress, yet still manages to crush whatever it lands on.

Bonezai's original design was a three-wheeled bike with an ejector seat that hurled the driver at an enemy. Chopov redesigned it to what it is now, and Samukai approved the new version, much to Bonezai's dismay.

WEAPONS:	Ninja slammer
CREW:	1
MAXIMUM SPEED:	300 mph
ARMOR:	Bone Plate
SPECIAL EQUIPMENT:	Elemental Mark IV engine

Becoming a Ninja

As my four recruits discovered, becoming a true ninja is neither easy nor as quick as one might like. In the time I had, I was able to give them the basics they would need to survive in a fight. But the training goes on, even as we pursue the Four Weapons of Spinjitzu. Truly, a ninja can never stop learning and improving.

Here are merely a few of the things I taught my ninja before their battles began:

Know Your Skills

Speed, agility, and instincts matter just as much as strength. A pair of rapidly rotating axes block the ninja's path. He must determine their pattern, time the gaps, and use his natural skill to evade their strikes. A most painful lesson, indeed, for those who fall short.

Know Your Enemy

You may be a master of every known martial art, but are you a master of your foe? You must study him, understand his drives and motivations, think as he thinks, and feel as he feels. Sometimes, this can be most distasteful, especially when your foe is an unliving skeleton warrior. But do it well, and you will be able to predict his moves almost before he makes them.

Know Your Land

A ninja must be one with his environment. That means knowing where the shadows will fall at any given time, knowing which direction the wind is likely to blow, and where an enemy might easily hide. It means accepting that a rock, a tree

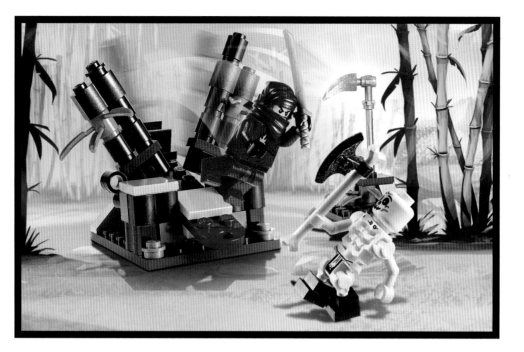

limb, a broken chain, are not just decorative features of your surroundings, but potential weapons in your hands.

Know Your Silence

Stealth and shadow are your allies when you are a ninja. The warrior who strikes in silence can overcome an army alone. Make a noise, betray your location before you are ready, and you will know nothing but defeat. To illustrate this, my ninja must make their way past walls lined with hidden axes and spears designed to emerge at the slightest sound.

Know of Patience

When your goal is before you, that is when you must stop, wait, and be certain of your next move. Many a battle has been lost in the final moments, when the warrior strikes too soon. Do not be carried away by the nearness of victory. Behave always as if a vast ocean separates you from your destination and you will reach it in the proper time.

Know What is Real

The innocent maiden in distress may be bait for a cunning trap . . . the solid, stable floor in front of you may conceal a trapdoor . . . the suit of ancient armor may conceal a foe waiting to strike. Do not assume that what you see with your eyes is reality. Reach out with all your senses, for appearances cannot be trusted.

Know Your Power

Once you have mastered Spinjitzu, it will be tempting to use it on many occasions. This would be an error. The man seeking to swat an insect does not use a cannon for the task. Save your power for when it will truly be needed.

There are many more lessons, of course—but just as important as what one teaches is how one teaches it. If you would train a ninja someday, you must keep these rules in mind:

1) Comfort is a thing of the past. A ninja will not fight his battles in a soft bed or in a warm bath. Ninja must learn to fight in every environment, from brutal heat to bitter cold, and so their training must include these climates as well.

2) To rush is to fail. Not only must a ninja know patience, but a ninja trainer must know it as well. Lessons must be given gradually over time, becoming more and more challenging as the warrior develops. To go too fast can be both frustrating and fatal for your students.

3) Moderation in all things. The ninja who sleeps too much or eats too much will be slow and lazy. The warrior who does too little of those things will be too weak to fight. A wise teacher will keep his students on the narrow path that walks through the center of life.

4) Calm before the storm. Even in the heat of battle, a ninja should be ice inside. He cannot let emotions rule him. His strength lies in his ability to analyze and decide on the right course of action in the midst of a fight, as opposed to acting out of rage or grief. Let the enemy be fueled by emotion, and make the errors that come with that. A ninja must be greater than such things.

5) Discipline. One who wants to be a ninja must be organized, respectful, and industrious in all things. How one behaves in one aspect of life will also be how one behaves in all others. A ninja who in his resting hours is sloppy, lazy, and reckless will be the same in battle.

Spinjitzu

It is a power as old as time itself. It is a weapon, but not the sort you can hold in your hand. You might even say Spinjitzu is a state of being, one difficult to attain and almost impossible to truly master.

At its heart, what is Spinjitzu? If you were to see someone practicing it, you would watch as they whirled and whirled until they had become a tornado of elemental power. That tornado could move at tremendous speed, soar off the ground, and deal severe damage to opponents. I have seen entire squads of skeleton warriors defeated by one ninja using Spinjitzu.

Even those few who know of Spinjitzu's existence have many questions about it, some of which I will try to answer here:

1) Who invented Spinjitzu?

My father was considered the first Master of Spinjitzu, but whether he "invented" it, I cannot say. Perhaps Spinjitzu is not something that can be created, only discovered within yourself.

2) Can Spinjitzu be taught?

I cannot show you how to unleash the power of Spinjitzu. But I can teach you other disciplines that will allow you to open your mind and spirit, so you can find Spinjitzu within yourself.

I told my ninja that I would not show them how to do Spinjitzu, but that they must find the key for themselves. And so they did, in the heat of battle.

3) Is Spinjitzu dangerous for the user?

By the time one unlocks the power of Spinjitzu, he or she already has the mental discipline to use it without harm. (Someone who somehow started using it without any training at all in the martial arts would wind up severely dizzy, if not far worse.)

4) How long does it take to master Spinjitzu?

Even I, who have been practicing Spinjitzu for ages, do not consider myself a true master. As with anything worth knowing, there is always more to learn and explore. In a fight, Spinjitzu can be used like a hammer, but it is far better to exercise fine control. Yet it can take a lifetime, maybe more than one, to learn how to do this.

5) Do the ninja's enemies know Spinjitzu?

Sadly, yes. Garmadon is as skilled in the art as I am, and as part of his deal with Samukai, he taught Spinjitzu to some of the skeleton warriors. Fortunately, they are not as skilled or as disciplined as my ninja . . . yet.

The Four Weapons

The Scythe of Quakes

POWER: By striking the Scythe against the ground, one can cause violent tremors and earthquakes. Kai used the Scythe to defeat the Earth Dragon protecting the Weapon, despite my orders against doing so.

LOCATION: The Scythe was hidden within the Caves of Despair.

GUARDIAN: Along with the natural obstacles of the caves, the Scythe was protected by the fierce Earth Dragon.

NINJA NOTES: The Scythe of Quakes was the first Golden Weapon created by my father. He used it to help form the continents that exist on Ninjago today.

The Shurikens of Ice

POWER: Anything they strike freezes instantly. The ice created is incredibly hard and requires extremely hot temperatures to thaw. Its power is so great that cold radiates from the Weapons, even when they are not in use.

LOCATION: An ice fortress in the northern region of Ninjago.

GUARDIAN: Those who survive the sub-zero cold and the dangerous creatures who live near the Ice Fortress will have to contend with the powerful Ice Dragon.

NINJA NOTES: The power of the Shurikens was used to create the frozen northern and southern regions of Ninjago.

# of Spinjitzu

The Dragon Sword of Fire

POWER: Anything it strikes bursts into flames. Also able to shoot fire over long range, it may be the most powerful of the four Weapons. When Garmadon last attempted to steal the Weapons, this was the first one he seized.

LOCATION: Sheathed in stone in the Temple of Fire, located near the Forest of Tranquility.

GUARDIAN: Protected by the mighty Fire Dragon.

NINJA NOTES: This is the only Weapon that has a name connecting it to a creature. There is a legend that the Fire Dragon's power may have been used to help create it, but I have no idea if that is truth or myth.

The Nunchuks of Lightning

POWER: Able to unleash sizzling bolts of lightning, powerful enough to shatter stone.

LOCATION: A floating city suspended over the edge of the world.

GUARDIAN: Its location is already extremely hard to access, but if one makes it there and attempts to take the Weapon, the Lightning Dragon immediately attacks.

NINJA NOTES: Dangerous even to touch, due to their electric nature, they can do harm to anyone who does not have a natural affinity for their element.

LOCATIONS

The world of **Ninjago** is home to many strange, exotic, and dangerous places. Here are just a few that my **ninja** have dared to visit:

Sensei Wu's Training Dojo

Hidden in a remote location, safe from prying eyes, my training dojo is where I prepare my four ninja for the trials they will soon face. From the outside, it might look like a simple structure. On the inside, it is designed to test the skills of my ninja to their utmost.

The entire building is lined with traps, and many of them are extremely dangerous. Kai once questioned why there are so many swords, axes, and such rigged to do harm. My answer was that he and the other ninja are not preparing for a game. The weapons the skeletons will wield will be real, so the training must be real also.

But it is not enough. I must devise new exercises. I must make the training even harder, even if every inch of my dojo must become a treacherous trap for my ninja. If they make it through and defeat Garmadon and his skeletons, they will thank me in the end.

The Ice Fortress

Located in the far north, and accessible only by boat, the Ice Fortress casts its shadow over vast fields of snow and ice. Constructed in ancient times by my father, the first Master of Spinjitzu, it is the hiding place of the Shurikens of Ice.

The fortress is huge, with walls, floors, and battlements all hewn from solid ice. The sub-zero temperatures alone are enough to keep most intruders away. The structure is lined with traps for the unwary, from razor-sharp icicles that shoot from the walls to trapdoors that drop one into the frigid sea.

The area surrounding the fortress is filled with dangerous creatures like snow serpents and frost gators. The fortress itself has only one occupant, an ancient Ice Dragon, placed there by me to guard the Golden Weapon.

Kai's Village

Hidden in a small valley, Kai's village was long a place of peace and security. Although its residents—primarily farmers—were not prosperous, they had enough to eat and clothes on their backs; that was enough for them. Kai's father and mother settled here many years ago, opening a small blacksmith shop, 4 Weapons.

Unknown to all, the shop contained a secret. Kai's father had created a map of the locations of the Four Weapons of Spinjitzu and hidden it inside the banner of his shop. There it remained until Samukai's skeleton warriors attacked and stole it, kidnapping Kai's sister, Nya, at the same time.

Fortunately, once they had the map, Samukai's warriors had no further interest in the village and left it alone. I hope that one day Kai and Nya can return safely to their home, free from the threat of Garmadon and Samukai.

The City in the Sky

Even I do not know who created this very ancient and intriguing site. To reach it, you must travel to the end of the world and stand at the edge of the tallest cliff in existence. There you will find a chain hanging down from the clouds. Climb the chain and you find yourself in the long-abandoned city.

Who once lived there, and why did they leave? How does it float, and how has it avoided discovery by others for so long?

These are mysteries I have never solved. But it proved an excellent hiding place for the golden Nunchuks of Lightning.

The Weapon is protected by the Lightning Dragon, which dwells inside the hidden city. When first introduced into the city, the dragon did a lot of damage. Interestingly enough, it seems the city itself is self-repairing. Either that, or there is someone else there that eluded even me.

The Forest of Tranquility

One of the most peaceful and beautiful spots in all of Ninjago, the Forest of Tranquility is a heavily wooded area with abundant wildlife, food, and water. Over the centuries, it has been home to many of those who prefer to be one with nature rather than dwell in cities or villages.

It is a most unusual place. Life remains balanced here, despite the absence of any kind of predators. Although there is little rainfall, fruit grows on the trees and other plants thrive as well. It is difficult, in such a place, to imagine that the world is being stalked by skeletons from the Underworld.

Perhaps, in the midst of our adventures, I will make time to allow my ninja to rest in this place for an evening. It might well calm their spirits before our true battles begin.

The Temple of Fire

This is the hiding place of the Dragon Sword of Fire, and so will be our last destination as we seek to gather all four Golden Weapons. It is located in a clearing near the Forest of Tranquility, at the base of a great volcano. Inside, the chambers are filled with shadows. Glowing hot rivers of lava bisect the landscape, leading to a stunning lavafall.

The Temple of Fire is home to the Fire Dragon, placed here to guard the sword. The Weapon itself is sheathed in stone. The Fire Dragon sleeps in one of the lava rivers, its back appearing to be stones that can be used to cross the fiery stream. Try to do so and the dragon will surely awake.

I have heard dark rumors that Garmadon may already have

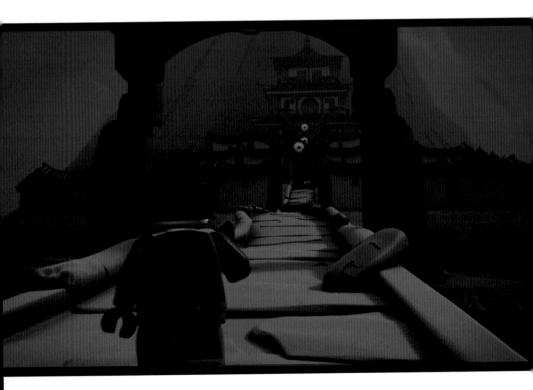

found this place and insinuated his power inside. If so, there may be traps within that I am not aware of and perils my ninja are not yet ready to face. But face them we must if we are to stop my evil brother. . . .

The Underworld

What is there to say about this terrible place? It is a realm of shadows and flame, of despair and hatred, filled with those who long to conquer Ninjago. It was with a heavy heart that I banished my brother, Garmadon, here, even knowing that the boundaries of the Underworld could not hold him for long.

There are, it now seems, multiple places where the barriers between the dimensions are so thin that beings can pass from

the Underworld to Ninjago and back again. However, only skeletons and dragons can do it easily or safely.

The Underworld is ruled by Samukai, the four-armed skeleton warrior. I do not know why he allowed Garmadon to build a fortress within his empire, or why he and his legions are serving my brother's interests. Only time will tell how long this alliance will last, but I feel the Underworld may never be the same when all is said and done.

Garmadon's Fortress

Although banished to the Underworld, my evil brother was not truly defeated. He waited and bided his time, building his power and constructing a mighty fortress in the heart of that dark place. From there, he made his plans to strike against Ninjago.

The fortress is well-defended. Skeletons atop the two towers man launchers that fire shadow missiles. Worse, a massive skeletal spider makes its home on the outer wall, launching itself against anyone who dares approach without Garmadon's permission. My brother sits on a throne of bone atop the fortress, but that throne is a living thing capable of flight.

It would be pleasant to think I will never have to see this nightmare structure in person. But though I am old, I am not a fool. Before this is over, I am certain that I and my ninja will have to face Garmadon on his terms and in his territory.

Ice Ambush

To truly understand **Ninjago**, you must enter the world. To learn more about the masters of **Spinjitzu**, read on, and discover more than has ever before been told about the recovery of the **Shurikens of Ice!**

ay stood at the railing of the sailing ship, staring out at the cold blue sea and the vast, white wasteland beyond. The bitter cold cut through his ninja garb and chilled him to the bone. He was doing his best not to reveal how nervous he was feeling. He had taken more than his share of risks in his life, but sailing through a field of icebergs made him feel helpless.

It didn't help that his teammate Zane was relaxing on the deck, seemingly immune to the cold. True, he was the Ninja of Ice, but here in the northern reaches of Ninjago it was icier than Garmadon's heart. Zane could at least

have the common courtesy to shiver once in a while.

"I spy something . . . white," Jay said.

Cole, standing at the wheel, shot Jay an annoyed look. "Could you try to be quiet for once? This isn't easy."

The Ninja of Earth turned back to steering in time to see a small iceberg looming ahead. Frantically, he twisted the wheel. The ship veered to the left, but the hull scraped the berg. Cole cringed at the sound.

"I spy something . . . broken," Jay said.

Nearby, Kai and Zane stood watching their mentor, Sensei Wu. The sensei had been standing on deck,

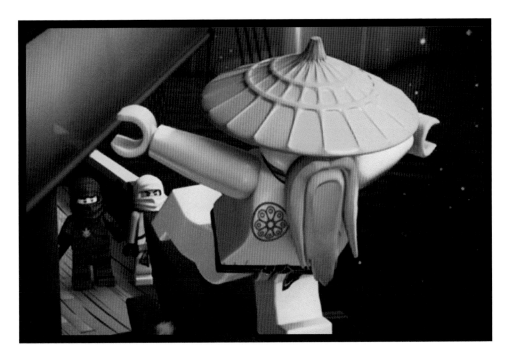

oblivious to the cold or the surroundings, engaged in a martial arts routine. He had once said the precise movements and ritual helped to keep him calm and focused.

Kai found he couldn't focus on anything but the cold. As the Ninja of Fire, this was not his preferred environment. "If the sensei knows the way to the next Golden Weapon, why isn't he steering the ship? We've been drifting aimlessly for miles."

Zane had to admit that Kai had a point. Although the team had succeeded in obtaining the first of the Four Weapons of Spinjitzu, the Scythe of Quakes, Sensei Wu had said very little about where the other Weapons could be found. Still, the elder must have had his reasons, Zane felt.

"Sensei's wisdom is beyond my own," he said to Kai.

Jay had walked up to Sensei Wu and was observing the martial arts master's moves. Noticing this, the sensei gave a slight smile. "Remember, Jay, the most powerful move in Spinjitzu can only be accomplished when all four elements are combined. Fire . . . ice . . . earth . . . lightning . . ."

"What happens when they're combined?" asked Jay.

"The Tornado of Creation," replied the sensei. "The power to create something out of nothing."

That interested Kai. He immediately began to mimic the moves he had seen Sensei Wu making. The sensei whirled with a stern expression on his face.

"No, Kai! If done incorrectly, it will lead to disastrous consequences."

"Disastrous consequences." Kai laughed. "Right."

The sensei took a step forward, but before he could act, everyone on the ship felt the already freezing temperature drop abruptly. There was a sharp cracking

sound. The team looked up to see that the sails had suddenly frozen. The ship was stopped dead now, run aground on an iceberg that had suddenly formed beneath it.

"That wasn't me," said Cole.

Kai looked down at his hands. "Did I do that?"

"No," said Sensei Wu. He pointed to a massive fortress in the distance, a citadel made entirely of ice. "We're here."

The four ninja climbed down the side of the ship and dropped down onto the ice. The footing was treacherous,

and Cole suggested they all hang onto each other to keep from falling. Zane offered to lead the way, since even cold this extreme didn't bother him.

They had gone only a short distance when Jay pointed at the ground. "We're not alone here, guys."

Up ahead, there were half a dozen sets of distinctive tracks in the frost. They were the footprints of skeleton warriors. Somehow, Samukai's followers had gotten here ahead of the ninja.

"They may already have the Golden Weapon," said Zane.

"Then we'll take it back from them," said Kai.

"They may be waiting in ambush—they're bone white, who could spot them in all this snow and ice?" said Jay.

"Think we can't handle them?" asked Cole.

"I didn't say that," snapped Jay.

"You should have," answered Cole. "Overconfidence has meant the defeat of more experienced fighters than us. Stay alert and let's get what we came here for."

Although the ice fortress had looked nearby when they were standing on the ship, in reality it lay across a vast field of snow and ice. The frozen ground crunched beneath their feet. The harsh wind blew fragments of ice that stung the exposed skin of the ninja. There was no sign of anything else, living or dead. All was still and white.

"You have to say this for the sensei," said Jay. "He takes us to the nicest places."

"It makes perfect sense that, if the sensei wished to hide the four Golden Weapons, he would do it in places that were inaccessible, remote, and/or dangerous," said Zane.

"I know that," said Jay. "It was a joke."

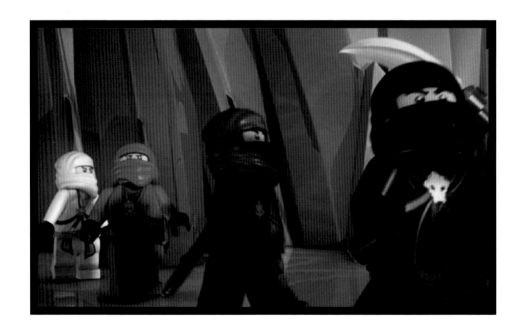

Zane looked at his partner, puzzled. Then he just said, "Oh," and kept walking.

"Hey, Cole," said Kai. "I think I see something up ahead. Looks like the snow was disturbed."

When they got closer to the spot, Cole pointed to the bones scattered around. "I think a skeleton was here, too. These belong to one of Samukai's warriors. There are signs of a struggle all over here."

"And five sets of tracks heading for the fortress," said Zane. "They abandoned their friend to his fate."

"I doubt skeletons have friends," Jay interjected. "I think hanging out and having fun pretty much stops when you're dead. Of course, if you're Zane, it doesn't happen much while you're alive, either."

"Quiet!" barked Cole. "Something's moving . . . under the snow."

Now they could all see it, the telltale shifting of snow and ice that said something was burrowing toward them. Zane pulled a shuriken from the folds of his robe. The others were still drawing their weapons when the ground erupted. All Zane saw at first were rows and rows of razor-sharp teeth in a great black maw. Then something

slammed into him, knocking him to the ground, and he could smell the foul breath of the creature.

Kai was already on the move, sword ready. He had heard of Zane's attacker, but never thought he would see one. Frost gators were said to be very distant relatives of Ice Dragons. They were reptiles that had somehow adapted to live in a sub-zero environment. They fed on land animals, birds, and anything else foolish enough to walk aboveground. Apparently, skeletons and ninja were on the menu as well.

Kai struck the beast with the flat of his blade, even as Cole and Jay landed flying kicks to its heavily armored hide. The gator roared and whipped its tail around, striking Jay and sending him flying a dozen feet. The creature crawled off Zane and headed for Kai, its claws digging into the snow.

"Yeah, come on, Gruesome," taunted Kai. "Next time, I'll use the sharp end."

Cole got Zane onto his feet, and Jay joined them. The gator had its back to them, its attention focused on Kai. The frost gator's preferred method of fighting was to force its prey down into the snow until it stopped fighting. It was feinting now, trying to find a gap in Kai's defenses so it could charge.

"Zane, throw your shuriken," urged Jay.

"No," said Cole. "Kai can win this fight on his own. He has the power."

The gator charged. Kai barely dodged in time. The frost gator hissed and tried to strike him with its tail. It clipped him on the arm, knocking him off-balance. Kai glanced quickly at his partners, shrugging as if to say, 'Where are you guys?" In response, Jay held up one finger and made a spinning motion.

Kai grinned. He took three quick steps backward and began to spin. In an instant, he had vanished inside a tornado of fire. The gator roared loudly and started to back away from the heat and flame. Kai whirled forward, driving the gator before him. Frightened, the beast dove beneath the snow and vanished underground.

The tornado died down and Kai tumbled to the ground. Jay offered him a hand up. "Nice one," said the Ninja of Lightning.

"Thanks," Kai said. Then, glaring at Cole, he added, "A lot."

Cole hid a smile. Kai might be angry now, but winning a fight on his own would give him the confidence to do it again later, maybe some time when the others weren't around.

In a matter of minutes, they had reached the castle. The huge door swung open easily. Beyond it was a long hallway. Cole was about to start down the passage when Zane shouted, "Down!"

All four ninja hit the frozen floor as ice daggers flew overhead from every direction. The barrage lasted a full minute. When the final frozen weapon had shattered against the walls, Cole lifted his head. "I think it's over."

"I sensed a sudden temperature drop," said Zane as the ninja rose. "I had a feeling it meant something bad was going to happen."

"You sensed a drop?" Jay asked. "From what: absolutely, totally freezing to absolutely, totally freezing minus one?"

Zane turned and replied, with a serious expression on his face, "Something like that, yes."

The team moved further into the castle, Zane now leading the way. Twice more, he saved them from potential dangers: one an ice deadfall, the other a trapdoor. The closer to the center of the castle they got, the colder it became, until even Zane had to admit his senses were being dulled by the temperature.

"Here's hoping we don't have to do much fighting," said Kai. "My hands are so numb I don't know if I could hold my sword. Someone needs to invent ninja mittens."

"And maybe some ninja blankets and ninja hot chocolate, while they're at it," agreed Jay.

"Numb hands or not, get your weapons ready," said Cole. "I think the central chamber is up ahead. If the Golden Weapon is anywhere in here, I'm guessing it's in there."

Weapons drawn, the four ninja cautiously entered the chamber. It was a vast, empty room, and felt much colder than even the outdoors. Hovering in the air, right in the middle of the chamber, were a pair of golden shurikens. These were one of the Four Weapons of Spinjitzu, whose combined power was sufficient to create a world . . . or destroy one.

"All right," said Jay. "Who else thinks this is too easy?"

"I'll bet they did," said Kai, pointing to the right side of the room. There, frozen solid in blocks of ice, were four skeleton warriors.

"All right," said Cole. "Just because it happened to them doesn't mean it will happen to us. Let's just get the Weapon and get out of here."

"Right," said Jay. "Four skeletons, four of us . . . no reason to think whatever froze them wants a matched set or anything."

Zane walked beneath the Shurikens and looked up. They were several feet off the floor. He jumped up but

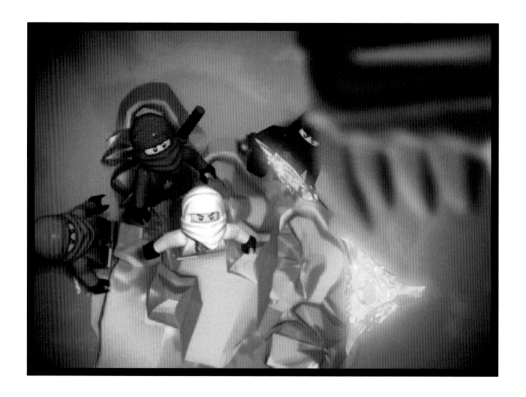

could not reach the Weapons.

The other three ninja hurried over. They hoisted Zane up toward the ceiling. Zane reached out and grabbed the Shurikens.

"I've got —" he began to shout. The next instant, his triumphant cry was cut off as ice formed all around him. Zane was frozen inside a ninja-sized ice cube!

The added weight of the ice threw the other ninja off-balance. Jay toppled over, the frozen Zane slipping out of his hands. Kai fell, too, but saw the danger as he did so. "Cole! Catch Zane!"

The Ninja of Earth scrambled to free himself from the falling bodies and caught the ice block a second before it would have shattered on the ground. "It's all right," said Cole. "He's safe."

"I'm glad someone is," Jay said, rushing to get back to his feet. "Look!"

Kai turned. The fearsome form of an Ice Dragon now filled half the room. Kai could feel its frigid breath and sense it was gathering energy for another ice blast.

"Amazing," said Cole. "There must be something in the room triggered by the action of touching the Shurikens."

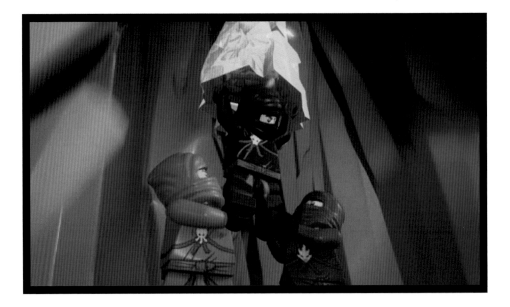

Jay grabbed Zane out of Cole's arms and headed for the exit. "Less analysis, genius, and more running!"

The three ninja and their frozen companion dashed through the hallways of the Ice Fortress. With a roar, the dragon pursued, shattering doorways as it forced its way through them.

"Hey, wait a second," said Kai. "I thought Sensei Wu left these dragons to guard the Weapons?"

"That's right," said Cole.

"Then how come they keep trying to kill us?"

"Maybe the sensei has an odd sense of humor," snapped Jay. "Let's figure it out later!"

The trio skidded around a corner. Jay slipped and almost crashed into the wall. Kai and Cole rushed to help him with Zane. The dragon was closing in on them now and any delay might mean the four of them would wind up as an ice pack.

"Come on!" yelled Kai. "We have to get back to the ship."

The dragon roared, sending a hail of razor-sharp icicles at the ninja. The three ducked as the frozen missiles shattered against the wall.

"You mean the ship that's stuck in the ice?" said Jay. "The one that isn't going anywhere?"

"Details, details," answered Kai. "Cole, get ready to whip up a tornado."

"What did you have in mind?" asked Cole. "I'm not sure if even Spinjitzu will stop that beast."

Kai looked over his shoulder at the pursuing dragon. "Maybe not . . . but could be something else around here can do the job."

The ninja shot through the main castle door and out onto the frozen ground, Jay in the lead with the frozen Zane. "Keep going," Kai said to Jay. "Cole and I will be right behind."

He turned to the Ninja of Earth. "Ready?"

"You bet," Cole replied.

The two ninja began to spin, faster and faster, until they had become whirling cyclones. The force of their motion lifted them into the air. Cole followed Kai's lead and both headed back toward the castle. As the Ice Dragon plowed through the final corridor toward the castle exit, Kai and Cole slammed into the archway above the door. Their tornadoes ripped through the ice blocks, bringing the entire front wall crashing down on the surprised dragon. Boulder-sized chunks of ice rained down on the beast, staggering it, as it roared in anger.

Kai and Cole veered off, slowing their spin, and crash-landed into snow banks. Kai brushed the snow away from his eyes and looked back at the castle. The pile of icy rubble was still, but he doubted it would stay that way for long — and once the dragon revived, there might be no stopping it.

The two ninja raced across the ice and caught up with Jay. The Ninja of Lightning was starting to struggle a bit, trying to run while carrying the heavy load of a frozen Zane. But there was no time to stop and chip their leader out of the ice. They could see the ship in the distance. The best thing to do was to get Zane to Sensei Wu, who would know how to help him.

Kai and Cole took the ice block from Jay and carried it together. "Oof! Someone needs to tell Zane to lose some weight," said Kai.

"Hey, I just thought of something. We need to get better at math," said Jay.

"Why?"

"There were six sets of skeleton warrior tracks, remember? We found one near the frost gator . . . four inside the castle . . ."

"That's five," said Cole.

"Give the boy a gold star," said Jay. "And five from six leaves one skeleton warrior still around somewhere."

"Right behind you," said a voice like a dead tree scratching against a window.

All three ninja slid to a halt. "He's right behind us," said Kai.

"So I heard," said Cole.

"Almost doesn't seem fair, does it?" said Jay. "One of him and three of us . . . of course, he probably has a weapon aimed at our backs."

"Or maybe he's a really big skeleton," Kai answered, smiling. "Maybe you should turn around and find out, Jay."

Jay did just that. A moment passed. Then he said, "Or maybe he brought some friends. What was that Cole said about overconfidence?"

Kai and Cole turned around. Instead of one skeleton warrior, there were three, and they were mounted in a fearsome-looking monster truck. The grill looked like a skull, the big tires were caked with snow and ice, and nasty looking weapons were aimed right at the ninja.

"Well," said Kai. "How did they get this here without us knowing?"

"Don't speculate," said Cole. "Heave!"

Cole and Kai hurled the ice block containing Zane and the Shurikens high into the air. For a split second, the eye sockets of all three skeletons were trained on the frozen prize as it flew skyward. Seeing an opening, all three ninja struck, fists and feet flashing as they charged the truck.

One of the skeletons started firing the truck's bone shooter, but the ninja were moving too fast. As the ice block reached the upper limit of its flight, Kai took out one of the skeletons with a hip toss. Then he did a backflip, landing on his feet in time to catch Zane.

Meanwhile, Jay was dodging another skeleton's sword, while Cole parried the blows of his opponent. Kai shouted Cole's name, then tossed the ice block at his foe. The startled skeleton saw the object hurtling his way a second too late. It struck him head-on, knocking him off the back of the truck, even as Cole leaped and caught the frozen package. Ninja and ice block landed

in the snow, both intact.

Jay was making progress in his fight now. A fast chop had disarmed the skeleton, and a sweeping kick was about to knock him off the truck. So Jay was pretty surprised when Kai ran, leaped, and grabbed Jay by the collar, yanking him off the vehicle.

"Are you crazy?" shouted Jay. "I had him beat!"

"I know, but I have an idea," said Kai. "Cole, come on— head for the ship."

The three ninja resumed their race for the stranded ship. Behind them, the three dazed skeletons revved up their monster truck and the chase began. Right away,

it was obvious that the ninja could never outrace the vehicle, especially not while carrying a heavy block of ice.

"I hope your plan wasn't us getting run over," said Jay.

"Just get ready to toss Zane to the sensei," answered Kai.

They were about twenty feet from the ship now, the truck right behind them. At Kai's signal, they hurled the ice block up onto the deck, where Sensei Wu caught it. Then the three ninja jumped for the ship. The monster truck roared forward, slamming into the hull of the ship.

The ninja hit the deck even as the ship shuddered from the impact. The entire vessel suddenly slid backward off the iceberg and back into open water.

"I figured all we needed was a little push," Kai said, smiling.

"What about the skeletons?" asked Cole.

"I think they have their own problems," Jay answered, looking over the rail.

Cole joined him. Down below, the weight of the monster truck had cracked the ice. Now the vehicle was sinking fast, taking the three skeletons with it.

"They should thank us," said Jay. "They're getting a bath and it isn't even Saturday."

A few hours and some gentle heat served to thaw out Zane and the Shurikens of Ice. The ninja now had two of the four Weapons of Spinjitzu, with only the Nunchuks of Lightning and the Dragon Sword of Fire left to be collected. But no one was celebrating. The skeletons had come painfully close twice to snatching the Weapons away.

"Where to now?" Kai asked the sensei.

"To the edge of the world," answered Sensei Wu. "The Nunchuks are up among the clouds . . . so I hope you are not afraid of heights."

Kai laughed. "After dragons, skeletons, monster trucks, what is there left to be afraid of?"

Sensei Wu didn't smile. "Let's hope, my Ninja of Fire, that you never find out the answer to that question."

And so, we have come to the end of our journey . . . for now. You now have the knowledge you need to adventure in the world of Ninjago, to battle Garmadon, Samukai, and their skeleton legions, and to help save this planet.

What does the future hold for Ninjago? I do not know. I can only be certain that Cole, Jay, Zane, and Kai will do everything they can to defend the weak, preserve peace, and protect the Four Weapons of Spinjitzu from those who would use them for evil.

Now I turn to you. Will you master Spinjitzu? Will you use your skills and power to fight for right? Do you have the courage to stand against the dark? If you do, it is time for you to prepare to defend your village.

The fate of Ninjago is in your hands!